DATE DUE			
5-7	T		
5-21	1-6		
9-12	2-11		
2-25	3-17		
3-4	3-24		
4-15	4-21		
4-22	9-13		
4-29	1-23		
5-13	T		
5-7	2-13		
5-14	10-11		
9-14			
10-21			

736.9
NAK
c. 1

Nakano, Dokuohtei.

Easy origami.

Dokuohtei Nakano

Easy Origami

Translated by Eric Kenneway

Viking Kestrel

VIKING KESTREL
Published by the Penguin Group
27 Wrights Lane, London W8 5TZ, England
Viking Penguin Inc., 40 West 23rd Street, New York, New York 10010, USA
Penguin Books Australia Ltd, Ringwood, Victoria, Australia
Penguin Books Canada Ltd, 2801 John Street, Markham, Ontario, Canada L3R 1B4
Penguin Books (NZ) Ltd, 182–190 Wairau Road, Auckland 10, New Zealand

Penguin Books Ltd, Registered Offices: Harmondsworth, Middlesex, England

First published in Japan by Takahashi Shoten, Tokyo 1981,
under the title, *Origamikan – 1: Yasashii Origami*
First published in Great Britain by Viking Kestrel 1985
Reprinted 1986 (twice), 1987 (three times), 1988 (twice)

Illustrations copyright © Takahashi Shoten, 1981
This edition copyright © Eric Kenneway, 1985

British Library Cataloguing in Publication Data
Nakano, Dokuohtei
    Easy origami.
    1. Origami ——Juvenile literature
    I. Title   II. Yasashii origami. *English*
    736'.98   TT870

ISBN 0-670-80382-0

Printed and bound in Great Britain by
Butler & Tanner Ltd, Frome and London

About the author

Dokuohtei Nakano was born in 1929, in Niigata Prefecture. He graduated from Tokyo School of Art in 1952, and spent fifteen years as a schoolteacher before starting to study origami in 1965. He thought it would be useful for his art students to learn. In 1966 he started holding regular origami classes and introduced an origami correspondence course for students at home and overseas. Profiled in 1972 in the New York Origami Center's journal *The Origamian*, he received high praise and became active on the international origami scene. In 1979 he established the 'Origami Castle' in Tokyo, with the aim of making origami more widely known.

Contents

Introduction

Japanese people have long used paper in ways which seem strange to us. Traditionally their houses have windows made from paper, for example, whereas we use glass. They invented the umbrella, but made it from pleated paper, whereas we use cloth. At one time they even wove paper to make material for clothes. Over the centuries the Japanese have become experts both at making paper of various kinds, and at making things from it. One of the ways they make things from paper is simply by folding it.

The Japanese word for paperfolding is 'origami'. It's an English word too, now, and has been for about twenty years (so you won't find it in very old dictionaries). A number of books on origami have been published in English over those years, some good ones among them, but this is the first authentic, graded course by a Japanese teacher to appear outside Japan.

Here are instructions for over fifty projects, and nearly all of them are things you can use or play with. There are no really complicated models (most are described in less than ten steps) and the different ways of folding paper are introduced gradually, so that you can become familiar with origami techniques in an easy way.

All the models here are folded from squares of paper. In most cases you'll need just one square to make one model, but in some cases several folded 'units' have to be fixed together, and for these you'll need a little glue.

So you'll need plenty of paper before you start, and you'll find it most convenient to use ready-cut squares. Special origami paper, shaded on one side and white on the other, is available in large stationery shops, toy shops, art and craft shops and department stores. You can also find origami paper, imported from Japan, in Oriental gift shops; and you may find packets of bright paper squares which, though not meant for origami, are none the less quite suitable.

Of course, you can always cut your own squares (10 cm., or 4 in., is a handy size) from writing paper, wrapping paper and any reasonably thin paper. The paper you use doesn't *have* to be coloured on one side, although this does help to make the results look attractive. Don't be discouraged if you can't find quite the right materials to begin with; you can achieve some interesting results just by experimenting. Happy folding!

Some useful addresses

In Great Britain Origami paper is packaged by John Maxfield Ltd, 93 Broadway, Mill Hill, London NW 7. Look out for their packets in the outlets mentioned before.

If you do have trouble finding origami paper, or want to learn more about the art, contact the British Origami Society: Dave Brill, 12 Thorn Road, Bramhall, Stockport, Cheshire.

In the United States Again, origami paper is available in art, craft and department stores, and you can also obtain it from a mail order company, who will supply a catalog. Write to: Hammett, Hammett Place, Braintree, Massachusetts 02184.

For more general information about origami, contact the Origami Center of America: Lillian Oppenheimer (Director), 31 Union Square West, New York, NY 10003.

E.K.

First and foremost

To become good at origami, you must keep on folding. Fold something once – then fold it again, perhaps using paper of a different size and colour. If you've folded something in the wrong way, start again from the beginning with a new piece of paper, because if you make too many unwanted crease lines your work won't look neat when it's finished.

Make sure you understand the most basic points about origami, laid out below. Then, as you fold the models, you can get to know the other signs and symbols which are introduced gradually.

Origami paper has two sides: a coloured side and a plain side

This is the coloured side.

This sign means: 'turn the paper over'.

This is the plain side.

Now let's try folding the paper

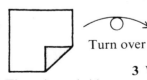 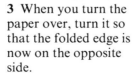 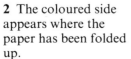

Fold line

Turn over

1 With the plain side up, fold a corner diagonally.

2 The coloured side appears where the paper has been folded up.

3 When you turn the paper over, turn it so that the folded edge is now on the opposite side.

Folding corner to corner

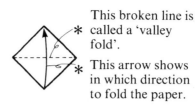

This broken line is called a 'valley fold'.

This arrow shows in which direction to fold the paper.

1 Make the crease as shown in the diagram. To do this ...

2 ... take hold of the bottom of the paper between your forefingers and thumbs. Raise the bottom of the paper, keeping your third and middle fingers inside it.

3 Place the top two corners exactly together with your forefingers.

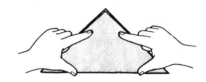

4 Still holding the corners together with your forefingers, make a crease along the bottom with your thumbs.

Firmly press the crease, using your thumb as an iron.

5 Are the two corners still exactly together? If so, press the crease once more.

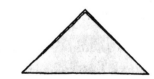

6 The two points are neatly folded together.

5

A useful tip to make folding easier

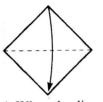 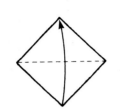 

1 When the diagram tells you to fold the top corner to the bottom corner . . .

2 . . . you can turn the paper round, and fold the bottom to the top, as described above.

3 It's easier to make the fold this way round.

If you take a look from the side at a piece of paper which has been folded in this way, you'll see it looks like a valley. That's why we call it a 'valley fold'.

It's all right to turn the paper round when you have to make a valley fold.

Making a crease line

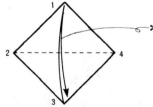 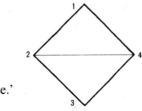

* This sign (an arrow which turns back) means: 'Make a crease.'

1 Fold the corner marked 3 to the corner marked 1.

2 Open the paper up. You've folded a crease which joins corners 2 and 4.

Folding an edge to a crease

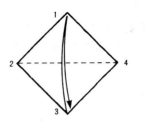 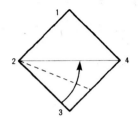

1 Fold corner 3 to corner 1; then open up the paper.

2 Take the edge 2–3 to the crease line. To do this . . .

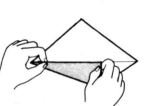 

3 . . . fold over the paper with your left forefinger and hold in place with your thumb. Take hold of the overlapping layer with your other hand and stretch it to the right.

4 Hold the corner in place with your left forefinger and make the crease with your right thumb.

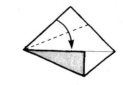 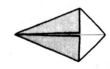

5 One edge is folded to the centre crease. Now it's easy to do the same at the top if you turn the paper round, as explained before.

6 Two edges folded to the centre crease.

Tumbling man

This is a traditional model which has been passed down from time immemorial. Just watch the tumbling man as he picks himself up again and again!

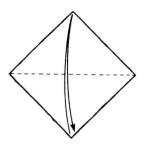

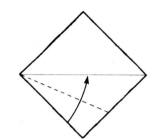

1 Fold in half; make a crease and unfold.

2 Fold the lower edge to the crease line . . .

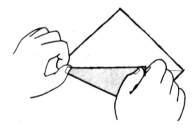

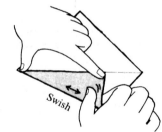

3 . . . and remember you can fold more neatly if you hold the corner with your left forefinger and stretch the edge of the paper with your right hand.

4 Hold firmly in place with your left hand and use your right thumb as an iron to make a smooth crease.

Swish

5 Make a similar fold in the top half, and remember it's easier to do this if you turn the paper round.

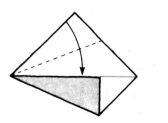

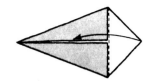

6 Fold the right corner to the centre.

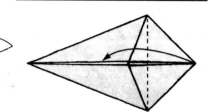

This sign means that the diagram or diagrams which follow are drawn to a bigger scale. Bear this in mind when you see it from now on.

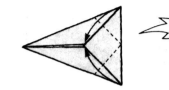

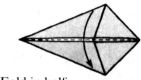

7 Fold the corners to the tip of the triangle.

8 Fold in the same way as step **6**.

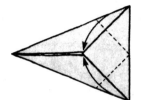

9 Make sure you fold as shown in the diagram.

10 Fold in half.

11 The tumbling man completed.

How to make him tumble

The number of times the tumbling man picks himself up will vary depending on the quality of the paper. Try making him from various sorts of paper and compare the results.

Lay him down gently.　Slowly he will start to rise.　Whoops! He's up.

7

Jumping frog

This paper frog also moves, leaping up when you press his back. He'll look even more real if you use green or brown paper.

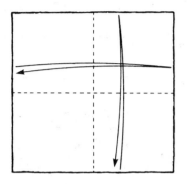

1 Fold opposite edges together in turn; crease and open up.

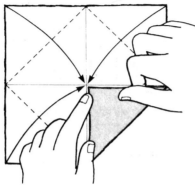

2 Fold the corners to the centre, turning the paper as you make each fold.

↑

> **Blintz fold** *Four corners of a square folded to the centre is called a 'blintz fold'.*

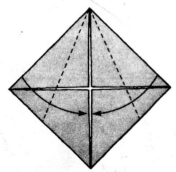

3 Fold the top edges to the centre line.

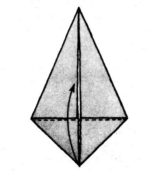

4 With the pointed end at the top, fold up the bottom triangle.

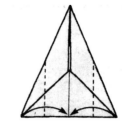

5 Fold both bottom corners to meet in the centre of the bottom edge.

6 It's easier to make this fold if you hold the paper in your hands.

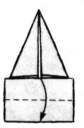

7 Fold down. .

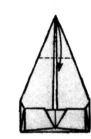

8 Fold his head.

9 Turn over.

10 The frog completed.

How to make him jump

A frog folded from a small square of paper jumps well. If you use paper 15 cm. (6 in.) square or more, repeat the blintz fold in step **2** and he'll jump well.

Press down on the frog's back with your finger. Slide your finger back

to let go and . . . boing! He jumps.

Crow

Here's another traditional origami design: a mischievous crow who pecks seeds from newly planted fields.

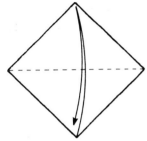

1 With the plain side up, make a horizontal crease across the centre of the paper and open up.

Thin lines in a diagram show you where creases have already been made.

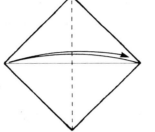

2 Do the same again to make a vertical crease. When you open the paper . . .

3 . . . you'll find creases in the form of a cross.

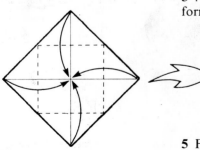

4 Make a blintz fold.

5 Fold two edges to meet on the diagonal centre line.

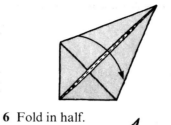

6 Fold in half.

7 Make the crow's head with a reverse fold. Place the fold a bit above the crease already made. This is what to do . . .

9 Draw back your forefinger; at the same time push down on the ridge of paper to change it into a valley fold.

⇒
Reverse fold *This is the sign for a reverse fold. Let's see if you can do it.*

➢
Fold to the side *This arrow tells you to fold to the side (not backwards or forwards). Here it tells you to fold sideways and downwards.*

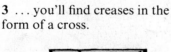

8 . . . Hold the paper below the fold line with your left hand. Insert your right thumb between the two layers and place your right forefinger on the ridge of the paper as shown.

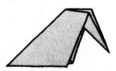

10 The crow completed.

How to make him peck

When you tap the crow's tail, he pecks for food. You can make a cawing, crow sound while you do this.

Pigeon

Pigeons are gentle birds which are very fond of corn.
You can make this model of a pigeon peck too.

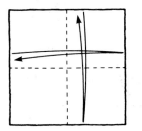

1 You already know how to fold steps **1-3** . . .

2 They form a blintz fold.

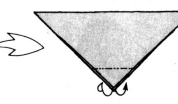

3 Now, take the top corner to the bottom corner.

4 Fold the bottom points inwards. To do this . . .

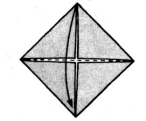

Fold both layers inwards
This sign tells you to fold inwards from both back and front.

5 . . . first, fold the front point into the model. Then, on the same level, valley fold the underneath point into the model.

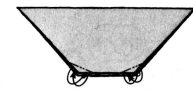

6 Fold the corners into the model.

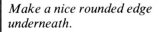

Make a nice rounded edge underneath.

7 Reverse fold to form the head.

8 The pigeon completed.

How to make the pigeons peck

Lay a sheet of paper on top of a table. Place two pigeons on it. Move the paper backwards and forwards, and the pigeons will peck in turn.

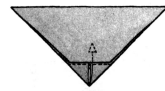

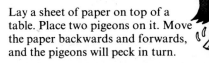

Hen

This hen could be sitting on a nest, warming her egg. She certainly looks very settled.

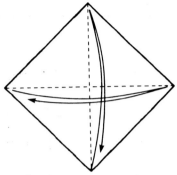

1 Make these creases and open up.

2 Fold the top and bottom corners to the centre.

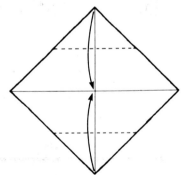

This hen could be sitting on a nest...

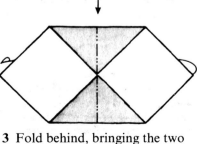

3 Fold behind, bringing the two corners together.

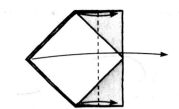

4 Fold the top layer only, at the point shown.

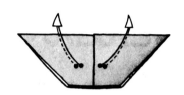

6 Hold the paper between fingers and thumbs at the points marked by black spots; and stretch the left and right sides upwards as far as possible.

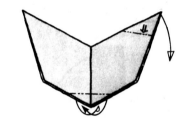

8 Reverse fold the head. To make the tummy, fold into the model from back and front.

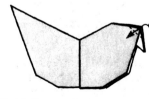

9 Fold the crest.

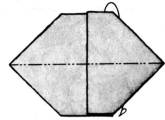

5 Fold behind, horizontally.

7 When you've raised the sides as far as you can, press the new crease at the centre.

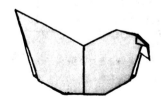

10 The hen completed.

Rat-tat-tat wrestlers

These simple shapes represent two Japanese wrestlers. Two people can play with them, or you can play by yourself and win to your heart's content.

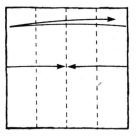

1 Make the centre crease; then fold the sides to the centre.

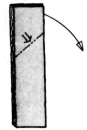

3 Reverse fold, making sure the outer edges of the paper are tucked in at the centre. The fold line meets the right-hand edge about one-fifth of the way down the column of paper.

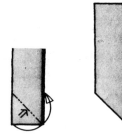

2 Fold behind.

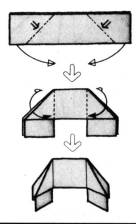

4 One wrestler is now completed. Make one more.

How to play

Draw a circle on a sheet of paper to represent the wrestling ring. Stand the wrestlers head to head in the ring as shown. Rap the table with your fists. The wrestler who falls or gets pushed out of the ring is the loser.

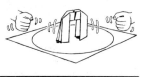

Building units

Start from the end of step **2** of the *Rat-tat-tat wrestlers*.

Pillar

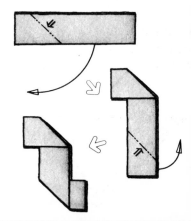

Use reverse folds to make a pillar, a foundation and a joint.

Foundation   *Joint*

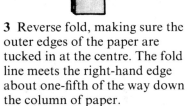

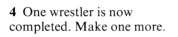

How to play

Try fitting these pieces together in any way you like to make new shapes. Join them to the rat-tat-tat wrestlers or step **5** of the floating boat (page 19). You can make things like a gate or a house.

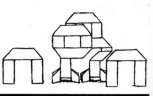

Talking masks
Alley cat

This is the face of a cat who opens and closes his mouth. It can be fun to play at making him talk.

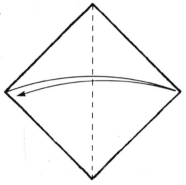

1 With the plain side up, make the centre crease. This line is important, so press it firmly.

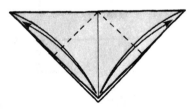

3 Make these two creases by folding the top corners to the bottom corner and opening up.

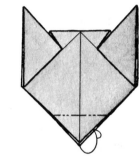

2 Fold the top corner to the bottom corner.

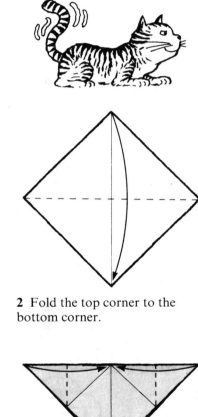

4 Fold the top left and right corners to top centre.

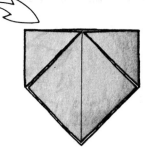

5 Turn the paper over.

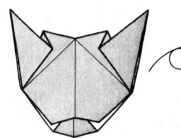

7 Fold the top layer only into the model.

The arrow with a broken line shows that the paper is to be folded underneath one or more layers. This symbol is often called an 'X-ray view'.

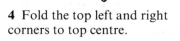

9 The cat mask completed.

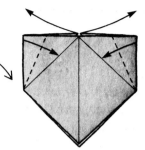

6 Fold the top left and right corners to the existing crease line, at the same time pulling the triangular flaps from behind to the front.

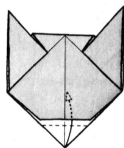

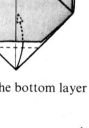

8 Now fold the bottom layer into the model.

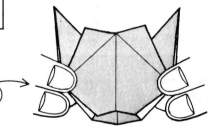

Look at the other side and you will see a bear's head. Hold as shown in the drawing and make the mouth open and close.

Talking masks

Pig

This is a pig mask, but with one or two alterations you can change it into a fox mask.

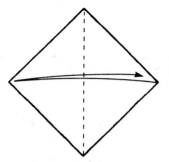

1 With the plain side up, make the centre crease.

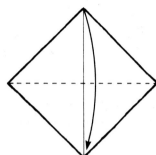

2 Fold the top corner to the bottom corner.

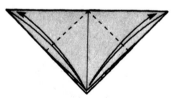

3 Make these two creases by folding the top corners to the bottom corner and opening up.

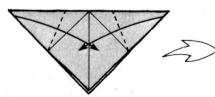

4 Fold the left and right corners down evenly.

5 Make these three valley folds.

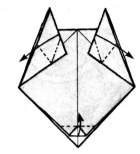

6 Turn the ears upside down. To do this . . .

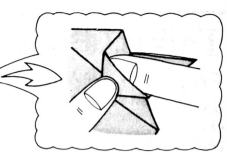

7 . . . put your forefinger behind the ear and, as you turn the ear over, flatten the ridge with the thumb of your other hand.

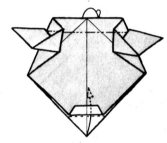

8 Fold the top edge behind with a mountain fold.

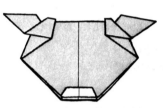

9 The pig mask completed.

Fox

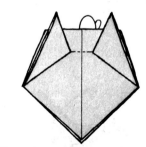

1 Complete steps **1–6** of the pig mask (above). Then mountain fold the top behind . . .

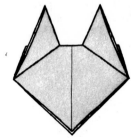

2 . . . and you have a fox mask.

Oink, oink

Talking masks

Frog

If you use just any sort of paper, will your model look like a real frog? Give some thought to the colour of paper you use.

Putting the crease lines in first makes it easier to fold from now on.

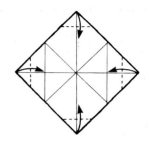

1 With the plain side up, make the centre crease.

2 Fold the top corner to the bottom corner.

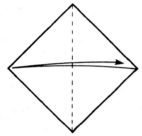

3 Fold the left and right corners to the bottom corner.

4 Fold the corners of these two flaps to the top.

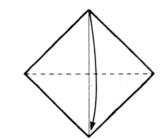

5 Fold up the bottom corner to make a little triangle.

6 Open up the paper completely.

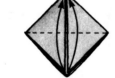

7 Fold the four corners.

8 Make the pairs of folds at top and bottom. Then fold the paper in half.

9 Fold the top left and right corners to meet at the bottom of the centre line.

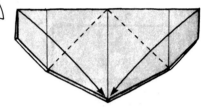

10 Fold up the bottom edges of these newly formed flaps.

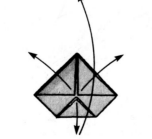

11 Reverse fold the bottom corners. Mountain fold the top corners.

12 Gently pull upwards and outwards to raise the eyes and open the mouth.

13 The frog mask completed.

15

Finger puppets

Dog

Here are some origami finger puppets. Why not make a puppet play, with everybody taking part? You can make up stories too.

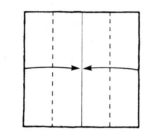

1 With the plain side up, make the centre crease.

2 Fold the sides to the centre.

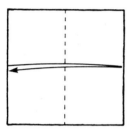

3 First make the valley folds (by folding the top edge to the left and right edges in turn, creasing and opening up). Then make the mountain fold where the valley fold creases cross, and then open up. Finally, collapse the paper forward by bringing the left and right edges of the mountain fold down to meet at the vertical crease. Squash flat the top triangle which is then formed.

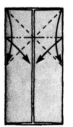

4 Mountain fold the top triangle behind.

5 At the top, raise the uppermost layers, squashing the concealed edges flat . . .

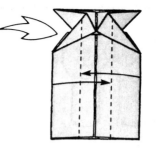

6 . . . like this. Now fold into thirds.

7 Form a pleat: first make the valley fold, then make the mountain fold.

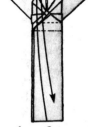

8 Fold the left and right ends of the pleat at an angle, squashing flat the concealed edges in the same way as you did in step **5**.

9 When you turn the paper over, you'll see that the basic finger puppet is completed.

10 Fold down the ears. Mountain fold the mouth.

> *The bottom will form a tube. Put your finger in here and wiggle it about to make the puppet move.*

11 The dog finger puppet completed.

Finger puppets

Cat, pig, cow, wolf

These finger puppets, of a cat, pig, cow and wolf, are
made starting from step **9** of the dog finger puppet.

Cat

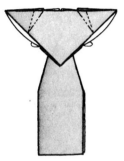

1 Start by completing steps **1–9**
of the dog finger puppet (page 16).
Turn over. Then form the ears:
first make the mountain folds ...

2 ... then the valley folds,
bringing the points up from
behind. Mountain fold the
mouth.

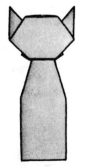

3 The cat finger puppet
completed.

*It's only the ways of making the
faces which are different.*

Pig

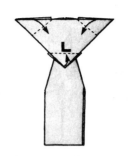

1 Start by completing steps **1–9**
of the dog finger puppet (page
16). Turn over. Fold down the
ears. Fold up the bottom triangle
so that it stands out.

3 The pig finger puppet
completed.

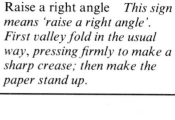

L Raise a right angle   *This sign
means 'raise a right angle'.
First valley fold in the usual
way, pressing firmly to make a
sharp crease; then make the
paper stand up.*

2 Flatten the point of the nose
to make it plump by pressing
between the layers at either side
of the point. Mountain fold the
sides of the ears.

Cow

1 Start by completing steps **1–9** of the dog finger puppet (page 16). Turn over. Then start to form ears by making mountain folds.

2 Valley fold the tops of the ears forward. Fold up the tip of the nose.

3 Flatten the nose as in step **2** of the pig (above) and the cow puppet is completed.

Wolf

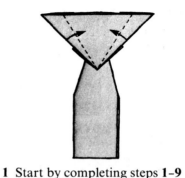

1 Start by completing steps **1–9** of the dog finger puppet (page 16). Turn over. Make valley folds which will form the ears and sharpen the jaws at the same time.

2 Make mountain folds at the top of the head, at the same time swivelling the tops of the ears behind.

3 Fold up the two edges and tuck them under the jaw.

4 The wolf finger puppet completed.

Floating boat

This paper boat may not last very long, but you can have fun floating it in the sink, or even in the bath. Why not have a boat race with your friends?

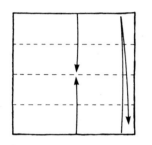

1 Make the centre crease. Then fold the top and bottom edges to it.

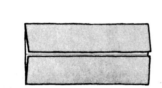

2 Turn the paper over.

3 Fold the four corners.

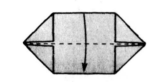

4 Fold in half.

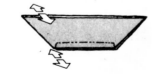

5 Pull the layers apart at the top, while pressing on the bottom to form the shape of the boat . . .

Pull apart *This sign tells you to pull two or more layers apart.*

6 (*top view*) . . . spreading two layers to one side and one layer to the other.

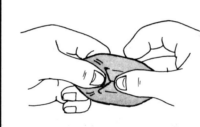

8 . . . and flatten the point with the other thumb. Repeat steps **7–8** at the other end of the boat.

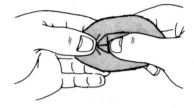

7 Turn over and make a crease across the seam at one end with one thumb . . .

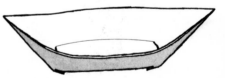

9 Round out the boat and raise the sides to complete.

How to float your boat

One side of the boat is heavier than the other, so add weight to stop it listing. Putting in a small coin will be enough to keep it steady.

Motor boat

Motor boats roar as they pick up speed, cutting through the water and raising lots of white spray. You'll have to make the sound effects for this boat yourself.

1 Mountain fold the centre crease. Then mountain fold the top and bottom edges to the centre behind.

⟹

Pull out   *This arrow tells you to pull out paper from behind or from within the model.*

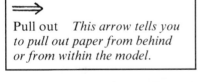

5 Make the vertical centre crease; then the quarter-line creases (by mountain folding the left and right edges to the centre). Then valley fold the left and right edges to the quarter-lines.

2 Take the folded edges to the centre crease.

3 Pull out the paper from behind.

4 Turn over.

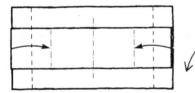

6 Fold the top and bottom edges to the centre crease.

7 Fold all four corners into triangular flaps.

8 At one end only, fold the sloping edges to the centre line.

9 Turn the paper over.

This is the front end.

10 Put your thumbs in the central pocket and pull apart to raise the sides of the boat. Pinch the mountain folds at right, when the sides are raised, to form the rear of the boat.

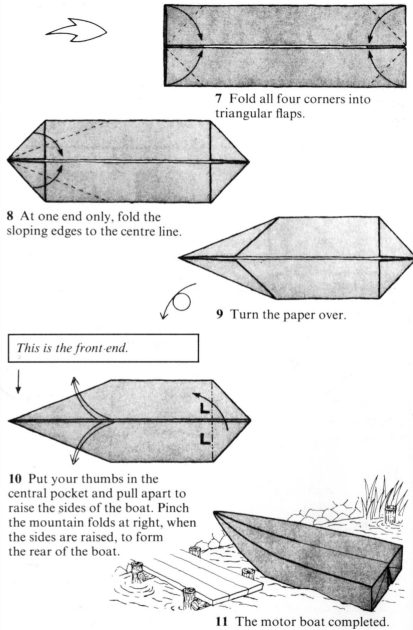

11 The motor boat completed.

Butterfly (1)

You can use brightly coloured paper to make a lovely vivid butterfly. If you like, you could even paint markings on the butterfly's wings – find a reference book to guide you.

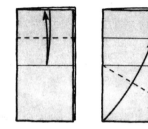

1 After making the horizontal centre crease, fold in half from left to right.

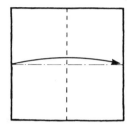

4 Fold the top part down, across the sloping edge.

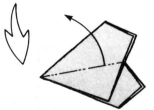

5 Squash fold, which will give you a mountain fold at the point shown in the diagram. Look at the following diagram to see how it's done.

2 Fold the top edge to the centre, crease and open up.

3 Fold the bottom left corner to the top right edge of the crease made in step **2**.

Folding into thirds *Steps* **1–5** *show one way of folding paper into thirds. This is something worth keeping in mind.*

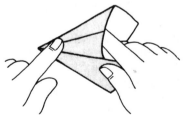

6 Raise the uppermost flap and poke your right forefinger into the pocket to spread the sides. Flatten the ridge of the flap in line with the folded edge underneath.

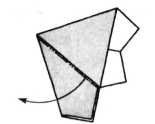

7 Pull out the lower flap and squash fold this in a similar way.

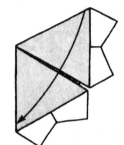

8 Then fold in half.

10 Press firmly; then pull the wings apart.

Squash fold *The method of folding shown in steps* **5–7** *is called 'squash folding'. Use your right forefinger, as in step* **6***, to keep the bottom part from unfolding.*

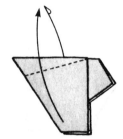

9 Fold upwards. Do the same with the flap behind.

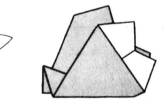

11 The butterfly completed.

How to make the butterfly flutter

Lightly tap the butterfly's head, as shown in the drawing. Its wings will flutter.

Butterfly (2)

If you have watched butterflies flying, you'll have noticed that they don't move in a straight line. This model flutters about like a real butterfly, and even turns somersaults.

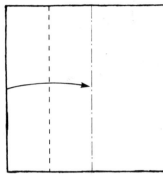

1 Make the centre crease; then fold the left edge to it.

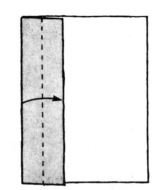

2 Take the folded edge to the centre.

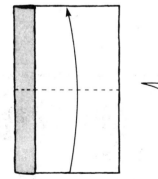

3 Fold the bottom edge to the top edge.

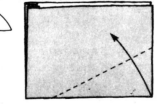

4 Fold over a set-square shape. The crease line starts at the bottom left where the paper thickens.

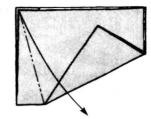

5 Separate and spread the two layers at top. This will raise the left edge. Flatten it, making sure the centre creases are in line ...

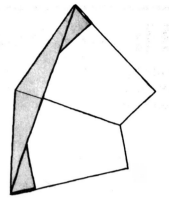

6 ... like this. You will have made a mountain fold along the line shown in the diagram for step 5. Turn the paper over.

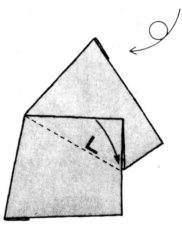

7 Raise the triangle, folded in step 4, to stand at right angles to the rest of the paper.

8 The butterfly completed.

How to make your model fly

Try launching the butterfly gently with the weighted front part hanging down. It flutters when it flies, doesn't it? If you turn it over and throw it like a plane, it somersaults and loops the loop.

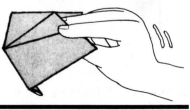

Hang glider

Hang gliding is a sport in which people soar across the sky hanging from gliders, which are rather like large kites without strings.

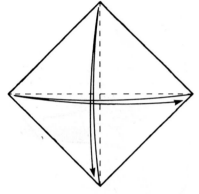

1 Make the centre creases and open up.

2 Fold one corner to the centre.

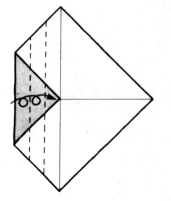

3 Make two folds, 'rolling' the paper to the centre.

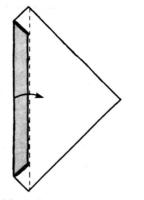

4 Fold on the centre crease.

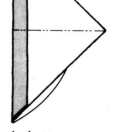

5 Take the bottom corner to the top corner behind.

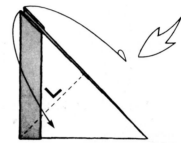

6 Fold the front flap forward and the rear flap back to stand at right angles to the main body. Pull the flap of paper at the front of the glider downwards a little.

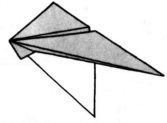

7 The glider completed.

Fold over and over in the same direction *This sign tells you to fold over and over again in the same direction. Make the first fold, then the second fold, 'rolling up' the paper.*

How to make the hang glider fly

The weight of paper at the front will balance the glider. Adjust the wings by curving them, and launch it.

Plane (1)

Paper planes are usually folded from rectangles, but the ones shown here are all folded from squares.

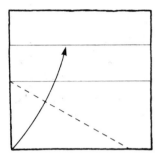

1 First make the centre crease; then the quarter-line crease at the top. Then fold the bottom left corner to meet the quarter-line crease. Take care that the fold line starts exactly from where the centre line meets the left edge.

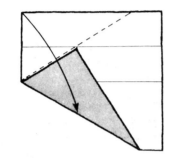

2 Fold the top left corner down over the sloping edge.

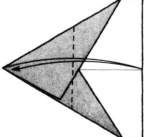

3 Make the centre crease by folding the left point to right edge of the centre line and unfolding.

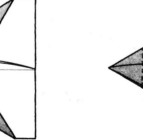

4 Fold the left point to the crease made in step **3**.

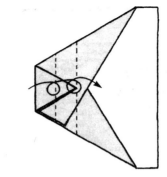

5 Fold the left edge to the point; then fold over again.

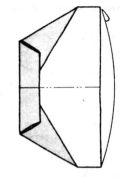

6 Mountain fold the bottom edge to the top edge behind.

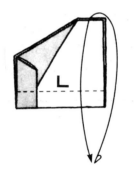

7 Fold the wings down in front and behind.

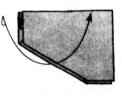

8 Make firm creases by ironing the top edges with your thumb. Raise the wings.

9 The plane completed.

Plane (2)

Let's make a plane with large wings. After you have made the standard model, try adding weight to the front and curving the wings. See the difference this makes to the plane's flying power.

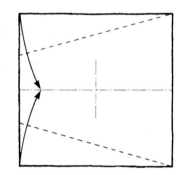

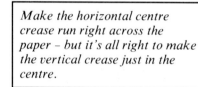

Make the horizontal centre crease run right across the paper – but it's all right to make the vertical crease just in the centre.

1 Make the centre creases. Fold the top and bottom left corners to the centre line.

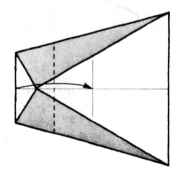

2 Fold the left edge to the centre ...

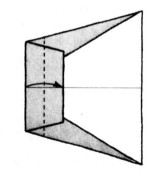

3 ... and fold again to the centre.

*If you want to add weight to the front of the plane, try folding the left edge over once more before doing step **4**.*

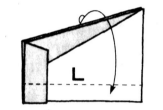

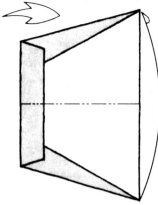

4 Mountain fold in half behind, from bottom to top.

5 Fold the wings to stand out evenly in front and behind.

The plane will fly better if you curve the back of the wings like this. It will prevent it crashing too soon.

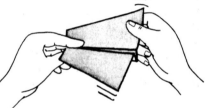

6 The plane completed.

Plane (3)

There are all sorts of ways you can fold a plane from a square of paper. This is a stylish plane with long and narrow wings. How does it differ from the previous models?

1 With the coloured side up, make diagonal creases in the paper (by folding opposite corners together and opening up). Then turn the paper over.

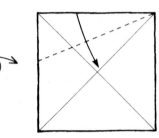

2 Fold the top edge to the diagonal crease.

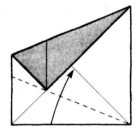

3 Fold the bottom edge to the other diagonal crease.

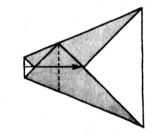

4 Fold on the existing crease line.

Don't forget to iron your creases firmly.

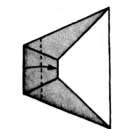

5 Fold again.

6 Fold in half behind.

To add weight to the front of the plane, you can make a further fold here.

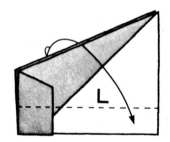

7 Fold the wings out level in front and behind.

Again, try curving the wings as shown in the picture, to make the plane more stable.

8 The plane completed.

Plane (4)

Fly your paper planes with friends in a park or other open space. See whose plane will fly furthest.

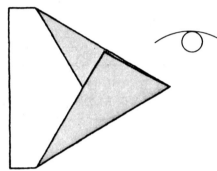

1 Complete steps **1-3** of *plane (1)* (page 24). Turn the paper over.

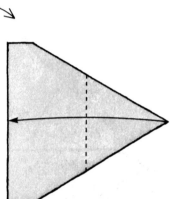

2 Fold the right point to the left edge. ·

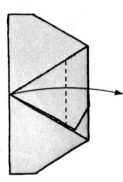

3 Take the tip of the triangular flap to the right, at the crease line shown.

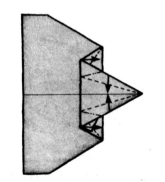

4 Now for a swivel fold. This is what to do ...

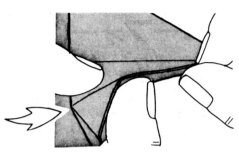

5 ... Take the top and bottom edges of the triangular flap to the centre crease in turn. The little valley folds at the side will neatly form themselves too.

> *When you fold an edge in a swivel fold, a second valley fold is formed naturally.*

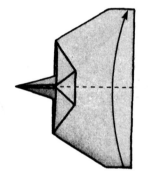

6 Compare your model with the diagram. Is it neatly folded? Now fold in half.

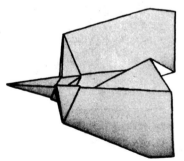

8 The plane completed.

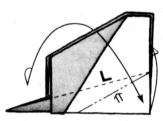

7 Form the wings by folding the flaps forward and back. Form the tail with a reverse fold.

27

Flying saucer (1)

You may have seen flying saucers in films, carrying strange creatures from other planets. Here is a space craft you can make yourself, using eight sheets of paper. It flies better if you make it from small squares of paper. Mind you don't hit anyone in the eye if you throw it, though.

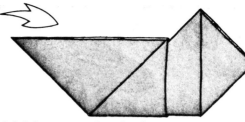

6 Make sure each point fits tightly into the pocket and fix it in place with a little glue.

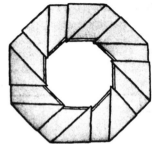

7 When you've joined up the eight units, turn over.

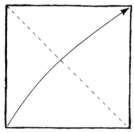

1 With the plain side up, fold the paper diagonally in half.

2 Fold the bottom corner to the top.

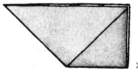

×8

3 One unit is completed. Make a total of eight units in the same way.

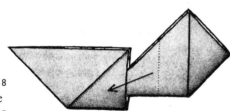

4 Tuck the point of one unit into the triangular pocket of another.

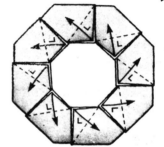

8 Note that there's an upper flap on each unit. Stand them up at right-angles.

9 When you've finished raising the flaps, turn over.

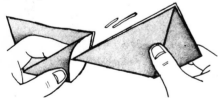

5 If you open the pocket by pressing down on the ridge, as shown in the diagram, it makes it easier to tuck the point in.

Fine dotted lines show how far to tuck in or overlap.

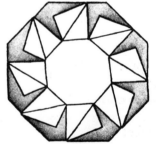

10 The flying saucer completed.

Flying saucer (2)

After playing with this flying saucer, you can tie thread to it and hang it up as a room decoration. You'll need eight sheets of paper.

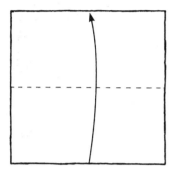

1 With the plain side up, fold the paper in half.

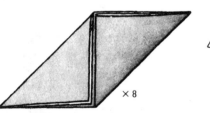

3 One unit is completed. Make a total of eight units in the same way.

× 8

2 Fold the top left corner to the bottom edge. Fold the bottom right corner to the top edge.

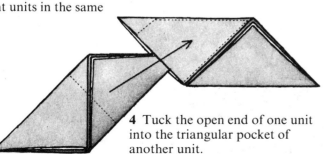

4 Tuck the open end of one unit into the triangular pocket of another unit.

5 Push it in as far as it will go and secure with a little glue.

> *Make sure you put each unit in the right way round, like this.*

6 Join up all eight units in the same way.

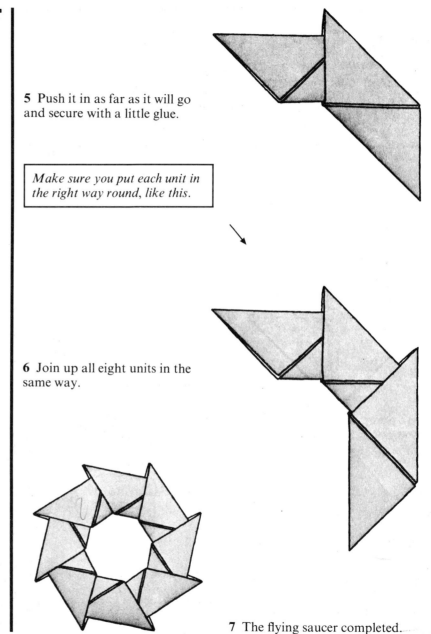

7 The flying saucer completed.

Flying saucer (3)

This flying saucer has a slightly more complicated shape than the other two. Again, you'll need eight sheets of paper to make it.

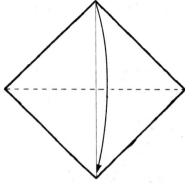

1 With the plain side up, make the vertical centre crease in the paper; then fold in half from top to bottom.

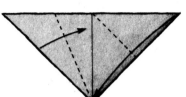

2 Fold the bottom left edge and the top right edge to the centre crease.

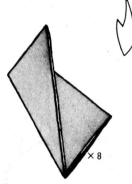

× 8

3 One unit is completed. Fold a total of eight units in the same way.

4 Tuck the point of one unit into the triangular pocket of another, as far as it will go . . .

> *Put the point right into the pocket and slide it up as far as it will go.*

6 Link up all eight units in the same way. Turn over.

5 . . . and secure with a spot of glue.

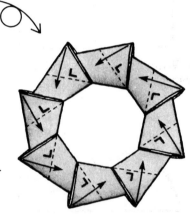

7 Raise the little flaps to stand at right-angles to the main structure. Turn over.

8 The flying saucer completed.

> *Why don't you try making your units from different coloured squares of paper, for a really bright effect?*

30

Flying saucer (4)

Here is another flying saucer which looks wonderful if you make it with different coloured units. You'll need ten sheets of paper this time.

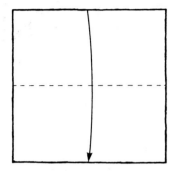

1 With the plain side up, fold the paper in half.

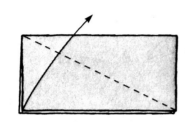

2 Fold on the diagonal crease line. It's easy to do this if you lay a ruler from corner to corner and fold the paper across the edge.

×10

3 One unit completed. Fold a total of ten units.

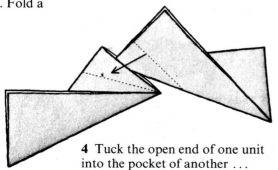

4 Tuck the open end of one unit into the pocket of another . . .

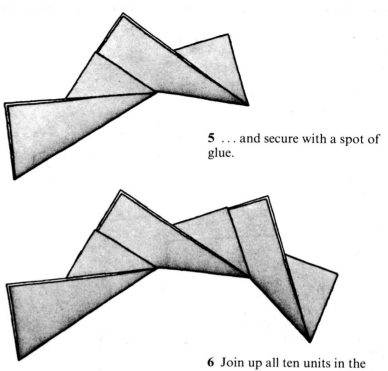

5 . . . and secure with a spot of glue.

6 Join up all ten units in the same way . . .

7 . . . to complete your space craft.

When you launch a flying saucer, flick your wrist a little to set it spinning.

31

Flying saucer (5)

Now let's fold a flying saucer which is curved like a bowl. You'll need five sheets of paper.

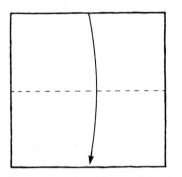

1 With the plain side up, fold the paper in half.

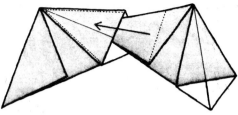

5 Tuck the pointed end of one unit into the pocket of another and glue.

2 Fold the top corners to the centre of the bottom edge.

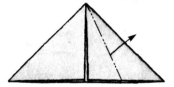

3 Squash fold the right flap only.

> *Remember, we used the squash fold when we made the* butterfly (1) *on page 21.*

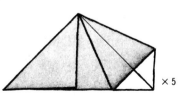

×5

4 One unit is completed. Make a total of five units.

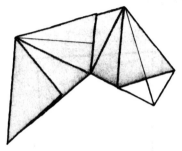

> *Curve the sides into the shape of a shallow bowl.*

6 Join the five units together in the same way.

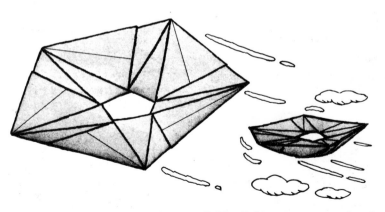

7 The flying saucer completed.

32

Wriggling snake

If you hold the snake's tail and wave it, he'll zigzag. If you make him longer, he'll coil up. You'll need fourteen sheets of paper.

Combine three sorts of unit:
- the head (one sheet)
- the body (twelve sheets)
- the tail (one sheet)

Head

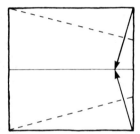

1 Make the centre crease; then fold the top and bottom right corners to meet it.

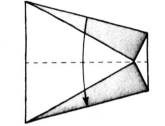

2 Fold in half from top to bottom.

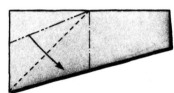

3 Make the centre crease; then squash fold at left . . .

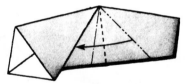

4 . . . and squash fold at right, bringing the mountain folded edge to meet the edge of the other squash folded flap.

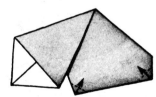

5 Form eyes by folding up the two corners.

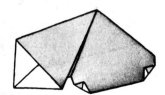

6 The snake's head completed.

Body

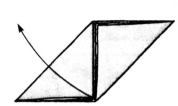

1 Start by making the unit for *flying saucer* (2), page 29. Raise the left flap.

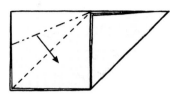

2 Squash fold at the left side.

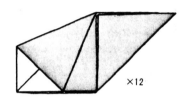

×12

3 One unit for the body is completed. Make a total of twelve units in the same way.

How to join up the units

Insert the folded point of one unit into the squash fold pocket of the next unit. Secure with a spot of glue.

Tail

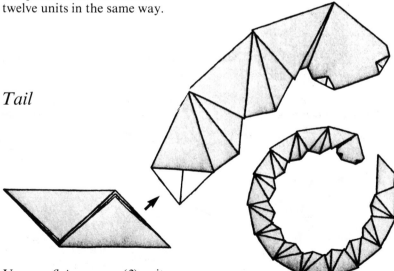

Use one *flying saucer* (2) unit, page 29.

The snake completed.

33

Ideas page
Bird and wreath mobile

You can make a lovely mobile by combining the *hen* (page 11), and *flying saucer* (*1*) on page 28. Hang it in the window to make a party decoration.

What you need

flying saucer (1)
hen
thread
needle
Scotch tape

How to make the mobile

1 First, pass some strong cotton thread through the centre of the hen.

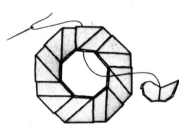

2 Next, pass the thread through the flying saucer.

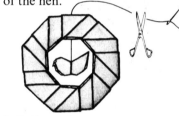

3 Pull the thread through so that the hen comes up to the middle of the flying saucer.

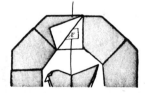

4 Then, fasten the thread with Scotch tape under one of the flaps to prevent it slipping.

5 Make a loop at the end of the thread to finish the mobile and hang it up.

'Leaf' bookmark

A leaf makes a pretty bookmark. There are leaves of various shapes and colours. See if you can invent a new leaf of your own.

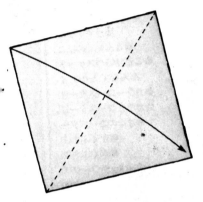

1 With the coloured side up, fold the paper diagonally in half.

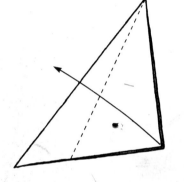

2 Fold over the top layer only.

> **Free fold** *Folds of the kind shown in step **2** are called 'free folds'. We have to judge their position by eye because there aren't always fixed points we can refer to.*

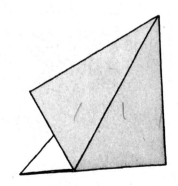

3 Turn the paper over.

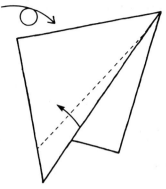

4 Fold the double-layered flap in half.

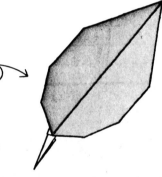

5 Make folds on three sides . . .

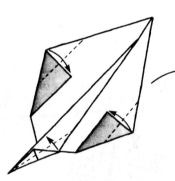

6 . . . and fold again. Turn the paper over.

7 The bookmark completed.

How to use your bookmark

Place the leaf between the pages of your book and let the stalk show above the edge.

When you fold steps **5** and **6**, try to be inventive. Consider what variations you can make to produce different leaf shapes.

35

Boots

You can make one origami boot to hang from a Christmas tree. Or make a pair of boots – tie them together with thread and you can hang them in the window.

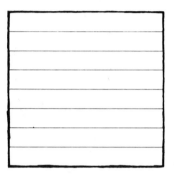

1 Make creases to divide the paper into eighths.

2 Roll up the paper, folding on the lines shown.

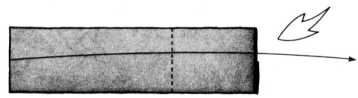

3 Fold on a line about two-thirds of the way from the left.

4 Fold in half behind.

Outside reverse fold
Separate the two layers, taking one to the front and one to the back; press down on the ridge between them to change it into a valley fold. A simple reverse fold, shown on page 9, forms a trough between two layers, but an outside reverse fold forms a trough around two layers.

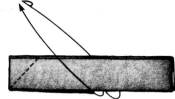

5 Outside reverse fold to make an angle, creasing at the line

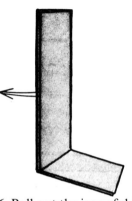

6 Pull out the inner folded paper to the left ...

shown on the diagram and leaving the underneath flap where it is. You will have to flatten the mountain fold line when you do this, but fold it back as a valley fold round the triangle of paper at the 'heel' of the boot.

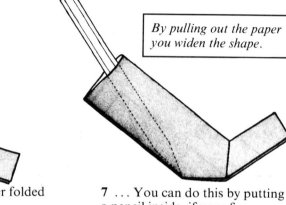

By pulling out the paper you widen the shape.

7 ... You can do this by putting a pencil inside, if your finger won't reach.

8 Form the foot by folding the bottom corners inside. Fold the top of the boot both backwards and forwards to make a crease.

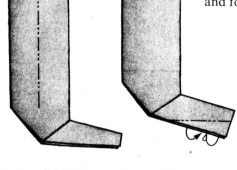

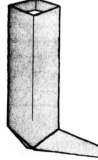

9 Then fold the top edges inside. Make the boot a bit rounded.

10 The boot completed.

Place card (boy)

When a lot of people are gathered together (at a party, for instance), place cards, each with a person's name on, are sometimes put round the table. They are to show where everybody is supposed to sit.

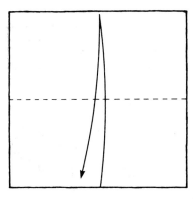

1 Fold in half, make a crease and open up.

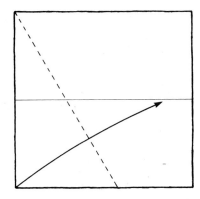

2 Fold the bottom left corner to the centre crease line, along the line shown in the diagram.

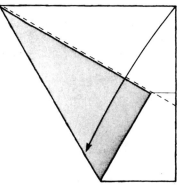

3 Fold the top of the paper across the raw edge to the folded edge. This divides the top left corner of the square into thirds.

How to fold into thirds *This is a different way of folding into thirds from that used in making the* plane (1) *on page 24. Make the fold right against the raw edge, pulling the top of the paper across it, for maximum accuracy.*

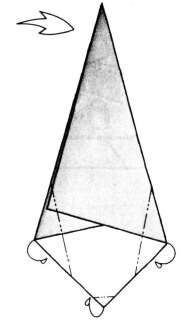

4 Fold behind.

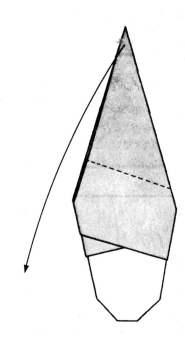

5 The face of a boy wearing a tall hat is completed. Fold the top point forward.

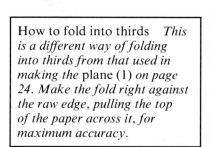

6 Free fold the top corner behind. At left, reverse fold the tip of the point inside; then make a valley and mountain fold to form the bobble.

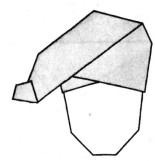

7 A boy wearing a woollen cap is completed.

Place card (girl)

Now let's fold a place card for a girl.

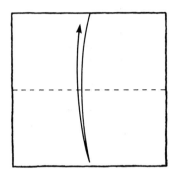

1 The first three steps are the same as for the boy's place card (page 37). Make the centre crease.

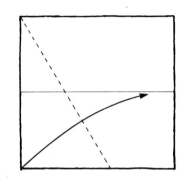

2 Fold the left corner to the crease line.

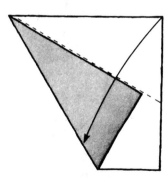

3 Fold the top edge down to the folded edge.

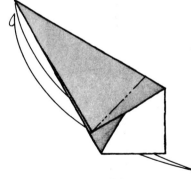

4 Mountain fold behind on the line shown. Make a firm crease and open up.

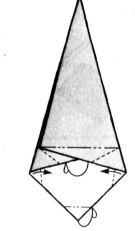

5 Fold the bottom corner behind to form the chin. Then swivel fold the top inside. To do this . . .

6 . . . push the coloured edges (below the mountain fold crease line made in step **4**) up into the model.

> **Inside swivel fold** *This is an 'inside swivel fold'. If you fold step **6** after having made a mountain fold, it's easier to do. Concentrate on making the mountain fold neatly and the valley folds at the sides will form themselves.*

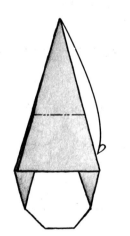

7 A girl wearing a tall hat is completed. Fold the point behind . . .

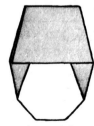

8 . . . to make a girl wearing a flat-topped hat.

Dustpan and brush

You can sweep up bread crumbs on the table, or odds and ends on your desk, with this dustpan and brush.

Dustpan

1 Fold the paper in half.

2 Fold up the front flap. Turn over and do the same behind.

3 Fold up the left corners . . .

4 . . . and fold again.

5 Turn inside out. To do this . . .

Turn inside out *These arrows, curving towards each other, mean 'turn inside out'.*

6 . . . open the paper until it looks like this. Hold as shown and press the ridges with your thumbs to turn them into valley folds.

7 The dustpan completed.

Brush

1 With the plain side up, fold in half.

2 Fold both layers together.

3 Fold the corner . . .

4 . . . and fold again.

5 Open.

6 Turn inside out by pressing against the raised corner behind.

7 The brush completed.

Box

There are all sorts of uses for a small paper box. If you turn it upside down, it becomes a stand on which to display your origami models.

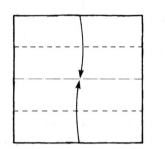

1 After making the centre crease, fold the top and bottom edges to it.

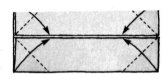

2 Fold the four corners.

3 Fold the left and right corners to the centre; make creases and then open up again.

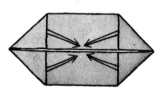

4 Raise the triangular flaps and pull out the hidden corners . . .

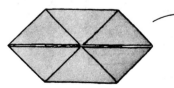

5 . . . to look like this. Turn over.

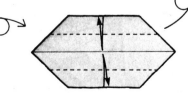

6 Make these creases; then turn over again.

7 Let's make a 'pull-to-perpendicular' fold. To do this . . .

Pull-to-perpendicular fold
This sign means 'pull to perpendicular'. It's a way of raising an edge instantly by squeezing paper on either side of a crease. The paper is doubled and the crease forms a ridge.

8 . . . hold the paper as shown in the diagram and draw the upper layers towards you. At the same time, push against the folded edge with your thumbs. The mountain fold crease line shown in the diagram for step **7** rises to form one side of the box. The near sides will start to form themselves . . .

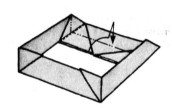

9 . . . like this. Similarly, raise the far side.

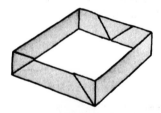

10 The box completed.

What to do with your box

Make two models and you have a box with a lid for keeping small things in. Use thick sheets of paper, one a bit smaller than the other. Or, the box makes a little cake dish, if you line it with a paper napkin.

Box of triangles

Look at this box from any side and you can see triangles. Folded in brightly coloured paper, it makes an attractive present. You'll need three sheets of paper to make it.

1 With the plain side up, fold the paper in half.

2 Fold the top corners to the bottom corner; crease and open up.

> *Have you folded the corners exactly and made neat creases by ironing them with your thumb?*

3 Fold the bottom corner (both layers) to top centre; crease and open up.

4 One unit is completed. Make a total of three units in the same way.
×3

5 Slide one unit into another to cover one little triangle. Glue in place. Join the third unit to them in the same way.

6 Then link up the three units like this.

7 Put a spot of glue between the open edges at the bottom of the box to complete.

> *You can make larger boxes by joining up four or five pieces of paper. But if you do use four or five units, cover the bottom of the box with a separate piece of paper.*

Bird basket

This is a neat box or basket in the shape of a bird. It can carry peanuts, or chocolates, or any little things that need tidying away.

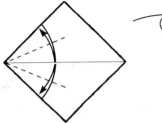

1 With the coloured side up, make the centre crease; then turn the paper over.

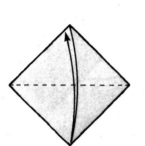

2 Fold the two left edges to the centre line; make creases half-way and open up.

> *Iron these creases firmly. They have a job to do later on.*

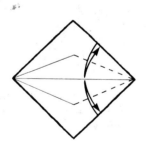

3 Fold the two right edges to the centre line; make creases half-way and open up. Turn the paper over.

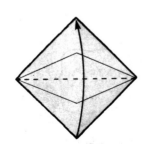

4 Fold the bottom corner to the top.

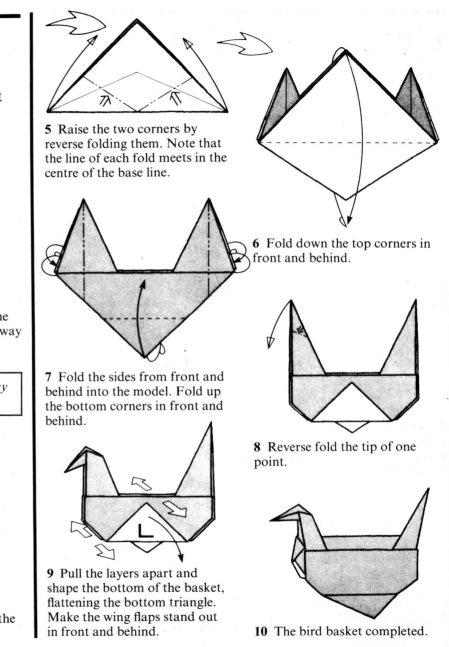

5 Raise the two corners by reverse folding them. Note that the line of each fold meets in the centre of the base line.

6 Fold down the top corners in front and behind.

7 Fold the sides from front and behind into the model. Fold up the bottom corners in front and behind.

8 Reverse fold the tip of one point.

9 Pull the layers apart and shape the bottom of the basket, flattening the bottom triangle. Make the wing flaps stand out in front and behind.

10 The bird basket completed.

Coloured table mat (1)

You can make a small mat, to stop your mug or glass making a mark on the table, or just for decoration. You'll need two sheets of paper.

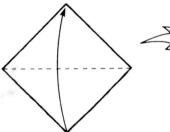 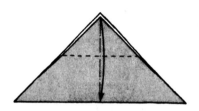

1 With the plain side up, fold the paper in half.

2 Fold the top corners down in front and behind.

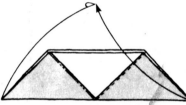 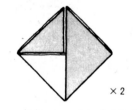

3 Mountain fold at left and valley fold at right to take the two corners up.

4 One unit is completed. Make a second unit from another piece of paper.

× 2

 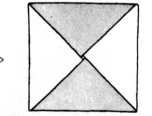

5 Slide the point of one into the pocket of the other. Do the same behind.

6 The mat completed. Turn it over and you'll see it has the same pattern on the other side.

Coloured table mat (2)

This mat is made from units which are slightly different from those used in the other one. You'll need four sheets of paper this time.

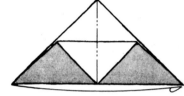 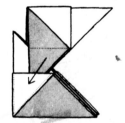

1 Complete step **1** of *coloured table mat (1)*. Then fold down the top layer only.

2 Fold in half vertically behind.

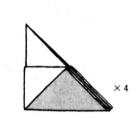 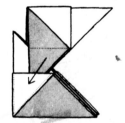

3 One unit is completed. Make a total of four units in the same way.

4 Tuck the two points of one unit into the pockets of another, in front and behind. Join all four units in the same way.

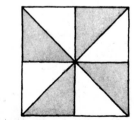

5 The mat completed.

> *You can hang this mat from a Christmas tree, too.*

Flower pot mat

This is a table mat which can be used to stand a flower pot on. It looks rather like a flower itself, so choose paper which has a cheerful colour. You'll need five sheets.

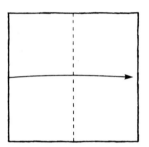

1 Fold in half.

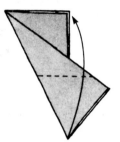

3 Fold the bottom corner to the top corner.

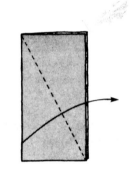

2 With the folded edge to the left, fold the diagonal crease.

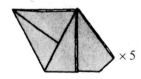

×5

4 One unit is completed. Fold a total of five units in the same way.

5 Tuck the point of one unit into the pocket of another, as shown.

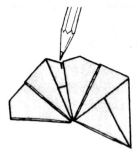

6 When the point is tucked right in, mark the edge with a pencil. Remove, glue the tip and replace.

7 Link up the five units in the same way to complete the flower pot mat.

If you've folded it neatly and tucked the points in as far as they'll go, you can use the mat as a flying saucer too.

44

Picture frame (1)

There are many ways to make origami picture frames.
This is quite a simple one, using four sheets of paper.
Think about the best way to trim your pictures to fit it.

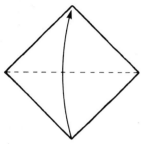

1 With the plain side up, fold
the paper in half.

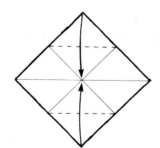

2 Fold the bottom corners to
the top corner.

3 Open up the paper.

4 Fold the top and bottom
corners to the centre.

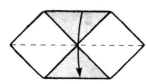

5 Fold in half.

6 Fold the two ends of the top
edge to the existing crease lines.

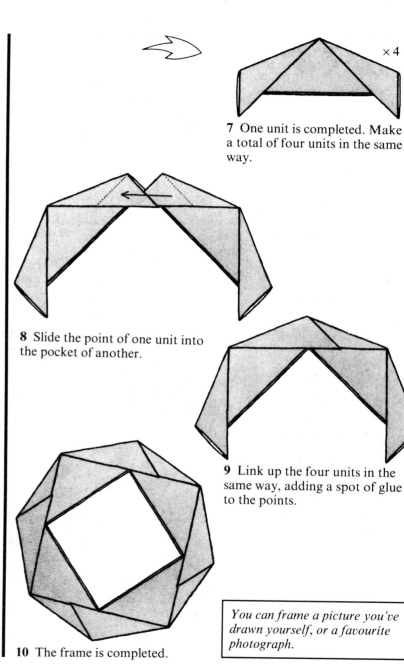

× 4

7 One unit is completed. Make
a total of four units in the same
way.

8 Slide the point of one unit into
the pocket of another.

9 Link up the four units in the
same way, adding a spot of glue
to the points.

10 The frame is completed.

*You can frame a picture you've
drawn yourself, or a favourite
photograph.*

45

Picture frame (2)

If you slightly change the way of making the units for *picture frame (1)*, you can make a square-shaped frame. Again, you'll need four sheets of paper.

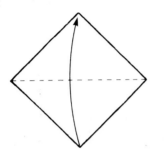

1 With the plain side up, fold the paper in half.

2 Fold the bottom corners to the top corner.

3 Open up the paper completely.

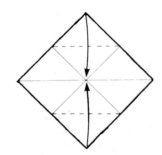

4 Fold the top and bottom corners to the centre.

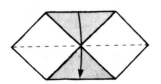

5 Fold in half.

6 Fold down the ends of the top edge to meet in the centre.

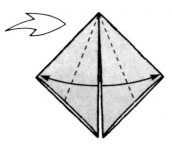

7 Fold the vertical edges of the flaps to meet the top left and right edges.

×4

8 One unit is completed. Make a total of four units in the same way.

9 Tuck the point of one unit into the pocket of another . . .

10 . . . like this. Join to the other units in the same way, securing with a spot of glue.

11 The frame completed.

You can have fun making your frame into a message board. Try and think of some other uses for it.

Paper patchwork (1)

Here is a piece of origami patchwork, patterned on both sides. You'll find it more fun if you and a few friends can make this together. You'll need twenty sheets of paper.

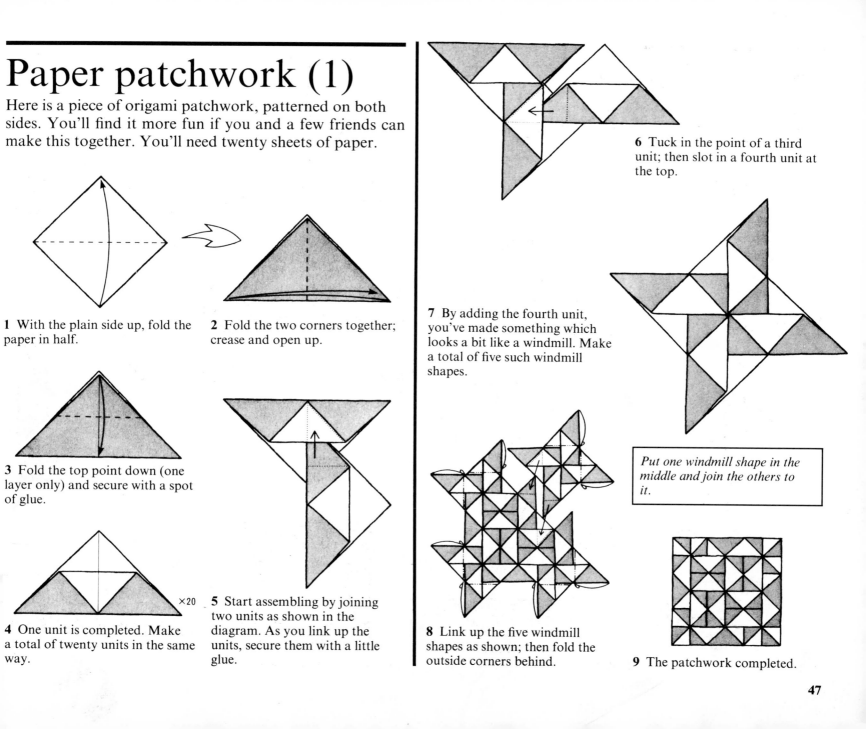

1 With the plain side up, fold the paper in half.

2 Fold the two corners together; crease and open up.

3 Fold the top point down (one layer only) and secure with a spot of glue.

4 One unit is completed. Make a total of twenty units in the same way.

5 Start assembling by joining two units as shown in the diagram. As you link up the units, secure them with a little glue.

6 Tuck in the point of a third unit; then slot in a fourth unit at the top.

7 By adding the fourth unit, you've made something which looks a bit like a windmill. Make a total of five such windmill shapes.

Put one windmill shape in the middle and join the others to it.

8 Link up the five windmill shapes as shown; then fold the outside corners behind.

9 The patchwork completed.

Paper patchwork (2)

You can make check patterns too. Join them together to make a wall frieze or a table decoration. You'll need thirty-two sheets of paper this time.

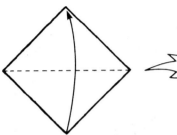

1 With the plain side up, fold the paper in half.

2 Fold the corners together; crease and open up.

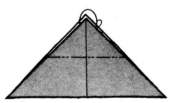

3 Mountain fold the top point (one layer only) into the model and stick down with glue.

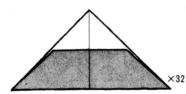

×32

4 One unit is completed. Make a total of thirty-two units in the same way.

5 Start assembling by linking four units to make the shape shown in the diagram. As you link up the units, secure them with a little glue.

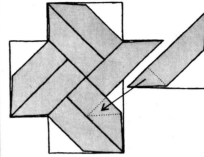

Build up the shape by tucking in units around the edges two at a time – lengthways and sideways alternately.

6 Join four more units round the central structure. The diagram shows three units in place with the fourth ready to be tucked in.

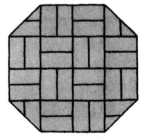

7 Join units, two at a time, to the main structure.
First, tuck units, two at a time, into each corner marked A.
Next, tuck units, two at a time, into each corner marked B.

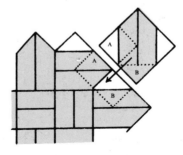

8 Join units, two at a time, to each of the four corners as shown.

9 Fold the corners behind, to complete an eight-sided patchwork shape like this.

48

Ideas page

Birthday card

You can make greetings cards by combining the *place cards*, on pages 37 and 38, with *picture frame* (2), on page 46. You could use them as birthday cards, Christmas cards – or what about as a Father's or Mother's Day card?

What you need

picture frame (2)
two place cards, made from
small squares of paper
square of paper
glue

Many happy returns

2 Write your message.

3 Take the place cards. Draw faces on them and write names on the hats.

How to make the card

1 Put the square of paper into the picture frame, sticking it down on the wrong side.

4 Stick the heads on to your card to complete it.

Try and think of some other ways you can use this card.

Sea bird

As well as paddling in the sea, the sea bird sometimes goes ashore to rest and preen its feathers. Try to bring to mind the feel of its beak, wings and so on, when you fold this bird.

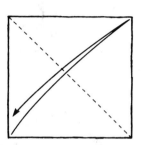

1 Make the diagonal crease.

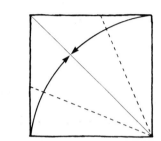

2 Fold two edges to the existing crease.

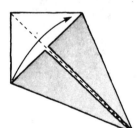

3 Fold the paper in half.

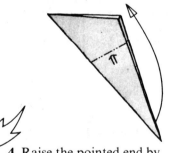

4 Raise the pointed end by reverse folding.

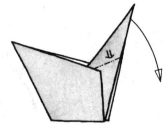

5 Then reverse fold down to form the head.

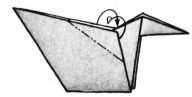

6 Fold the front and back corners inwards.

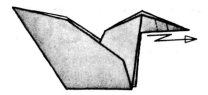

7 Form the beak with a double reverse fold. To do this . . .

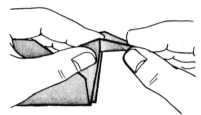

Double reverse fold (1)   *This is the sign for a double reverse fold. By folding the beak back and then forward, you make little triangles on either side to form eyes.*

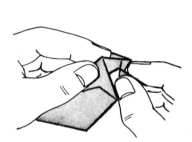

8 . . . hold the paper as shown.

9 Form a step in the point with the tip of your right forefinger.

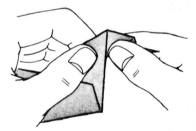

10 Press between finger and thumb to fix the new shape.

11 Fold the front and back corners inwards.

12 The sea bird completed.

Swimming bird (1)

Birds sometimes look for food while paddling along on the surface of the water. Have you ever seen them suddenly dive for food while swimming along?

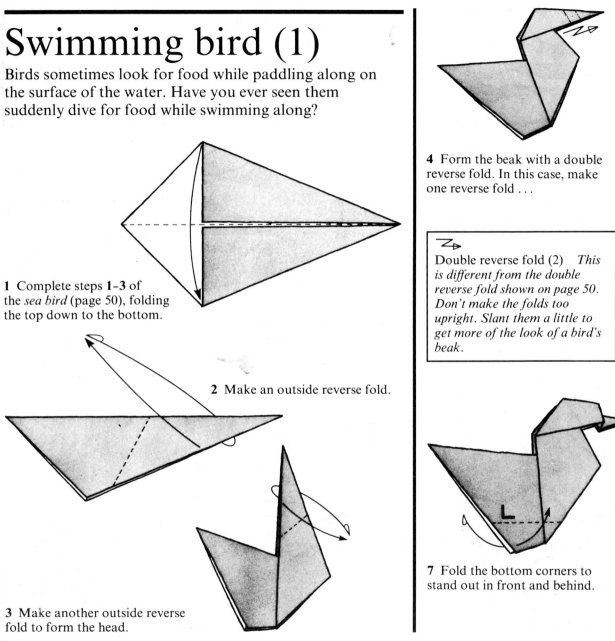

1 Complete steps **1–3** of the *sea bird* (page 50), folding the top down to the bottom.

2 Make an outside reverse fold.

3 Make another outside reverse fold to form the head.

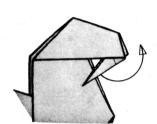

4 Form the beak with a double reverse fold. In this case, make one reverse fold . . .

Double reverse fold (2) *This is different from the double reverse fold shown on page 50. Don't make the folds too upright. Slant them a little to get more of the look of a bird's beak.*

7 Fold the bottom corners to stand out in front and behind.

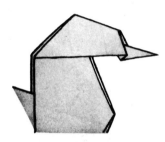

5 . . . and then a second reverse fold.

6 The beak completed.

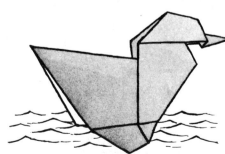

8 The swimming bird completed.

51

Duck

Ducks live on rivers and ponds. There are many different kinds, from the drake mallard with its bright green head, to the eider with its soft down.

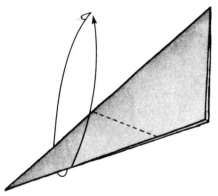

1 Complete steps **1** and **2** of the *swimming bird (1)*, page 51. Then make an outside reverse fold.

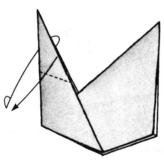

2 Outside reverse fold again.

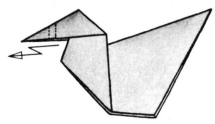

3 Form the beak with a double reverse fold (2), as shown on page 51.

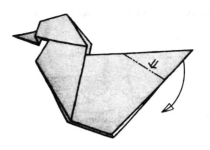

4 Reverse fold the tail down . . .

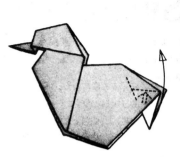

5 . . . and reverse fold the tip up.

Inside crimp *The way of folding a bird's tail shown in steps* **4** *and* **5** *is called an 'inside crimp'. Usually the two folds are treated as a single move, and drawn as shown here.*

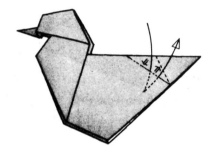

6 Fold inwards from front and back.

7 The duck completed.

52

Swimming bird (2)

Let's fold a bird which swims along with his neck poking forward, looking for insects to snap up. There's a special way of folding the beak in this model.

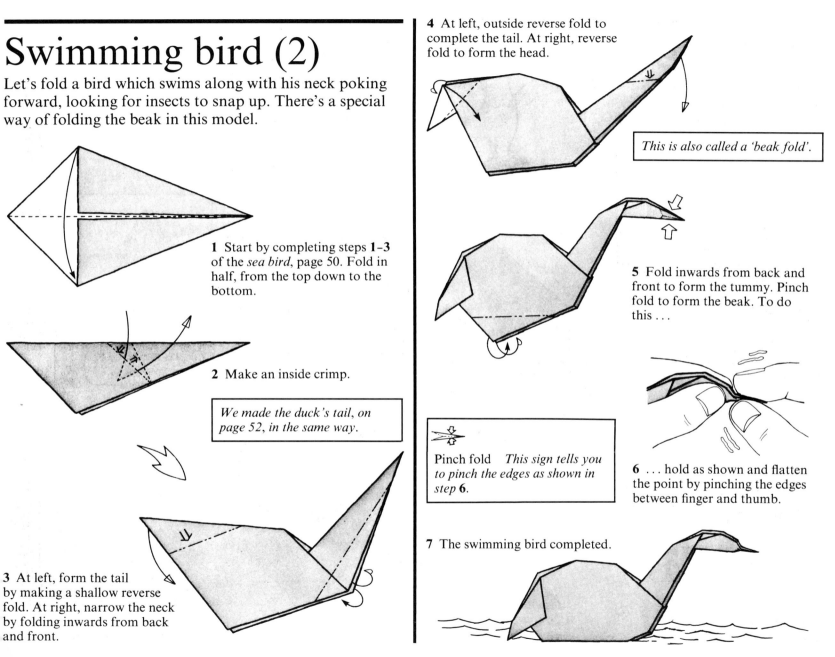

1 Start by completing steps **1–3** of the *sea bird*, page 50. Fold in half, from the top down to the bottom.

2 Make an inside crimp.

We made the duck's tail, on page 52, in the same way.

3 At left, form the tail by making a shallow reverse fold. At right, narrow the neck by folding inwards from back and front.

4 At left, outside reverse fold to complete the tail. At right, reverse fold to form the head.

This is also called a 'beak fold'.

5 Fold inwards from back and front to form the tummy. Pinch fold to form the beak. To do this . . .

Pinch fold   *This sign tells you to pinch the edges as shown in step **6**.*

6 . . . hold as shown and flatten the point by pinching the edges between finger and thumb.

7 The swimming bird completed.

53

Good dog

Here's a dog sitting patiently. He might be asking for his dinner, or waiting to be taken for a walk.

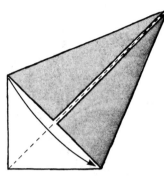

1 Start by completing steps **1–3** of the *sea bird*, page 50, folding in half from top to bottom.

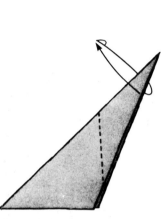

2 Make an outside reverse fold.

3 Once more, outside reverse fold.

> ⟪sink symbol⟫ ⇐
> Sinking a point   *This sign tells you to 'sink' a point. We do this in instances when we can't make a reverse fold.*

4 Sink the point to narrow the neck. To do this, first make a firm crease on the mountain fold line shown here . . .

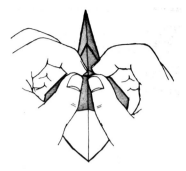

5 . . . then separate the two layers, like this.

6 Push against the point to make a hollow. Then pinch a horizontal mountain fold to make the base of a triangle of creases.

> *It's easier to make this fold if you take it slowly. It just gives a finishing touch to the neck.*

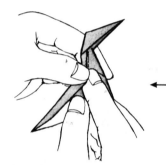

7 Make a hollow where the creases meet in the middle. Close the model and press firmly.

8 Form the tail with an inside crimp. Double reverse fold to form the nose.

9 Reverse fold the tip to complete the nose. Narrow the tail by folding inwards from back and front.

10 The dog completed.

Walking dog

This dog is out for a walk. He seems very happy trotting along with his head down.

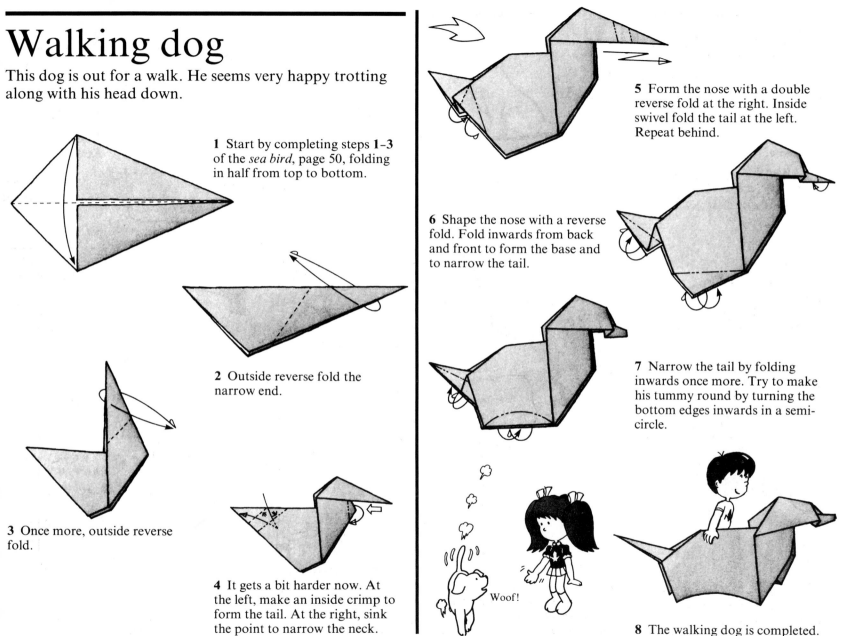

1 Start by completing steps **1–3** of the *sea bird*, page 50, folding in half from top to bottom.

2 Outside reverse fold the narrow end.

3 Once more, outside reverse fold.

4 It gets a bit harder now. At the left, make an inside crimp to form the tail. At the right, sink the point to narrow the neck.

5 Form the nose with a double reverse fold at the right. Inside swivel fold the tail at the left. Repeat behind.

6 Shape the nose with a reverse fold. Fold inwards from back and front to form the base and to narrow the tail.

7 Narrow the tail by folding inwards once more. Try to make his tummy round by turning the bottom edges inwards in a semi-circle.

Woof!

8 The walking dog is completed.

Sitting dog

Let's fold a dog sitting properly with his tail stretched out behind him. Fold him so that his tail lies on the ground.

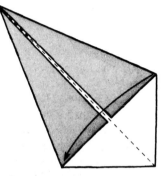

1 Start by completing steps **1–3** of the *sea bird*, page 50. Fold in half.

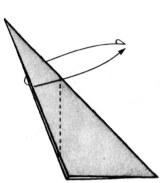

2 Outside reverse fold.

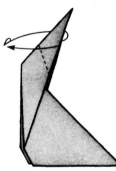

3 Outside reverse fold again.

Remember, sinking a point was described on page 54.

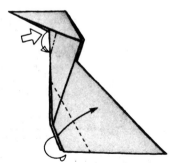

4 Sink the point of the neck. Fold the bottom left layers to back and front.

5 To straighten the edges of these flaps at front and back, make inside swivel folds as shown in step **6**.

Remember, we made an inside swivel fold for the place card on page 38.

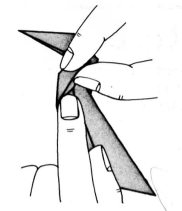

6 Make a mountain fold and push the surplus paper behind it. Do the same behind.

7 Double reverse fold the nose. Make a crimp for the tail. Fold the flap at left to form a leg. Repeat behind.

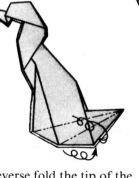

Woof!

8 Reverse fold the tip of the nose. At bottom, fold each layer in turn over and over into the model.

9 The sitting dog completed.

56

Rose

Roses come in many colours. Which is your favourite? You could fold a whole bed of roses, in pink, red and yellow papers. You'll need six sheets for each one.

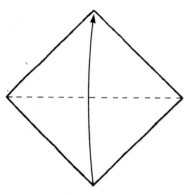

1 With the plain side up, fold in half.

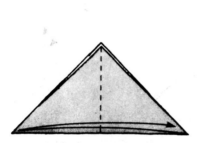

2 Fold both corners together; crease and open up.

3 Fold the bottom corners to the top corner.

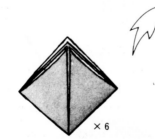

×6

4 One unit is completed. Fold a total of six units in the same way.

5 On each unit, overlap the two front flaps and glue them together. This makes the flat unit into a cone shape.

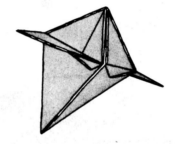

7 Glue two units together as shown. Then join on the remaining units.

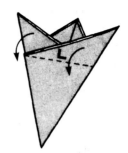

6 Fold the overlapped corners of each unit forward.

To make a decoration, push a drinking straw in between the edges underneath the flower. Fix on an origami butterfly (made with a small square of paper) and stand it in a glass. Make lots of flowers for a really good display.

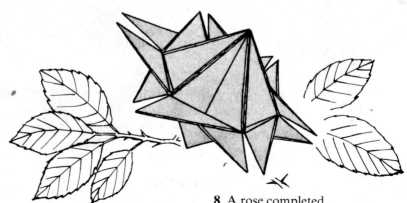

8 A rose completed.

Gentian

Gentians are beautiful plants with long, trumpet-shaped flowers, that are usually a lovely deep blue. See if you can find some vivid paper to fold them in. You'll need six sheets for each flower.

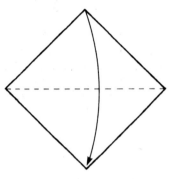

1 With the plain side up, fold in half.

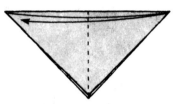

2 Fold the top corners together and open up to make the vertical crease.

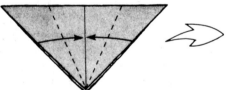

3 Fold the left and right edges to the vertical crease.

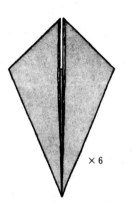

×6

4 One unit completed. Make a total of six units in the same way.

This unit is longer and narrower than the one for the rose.

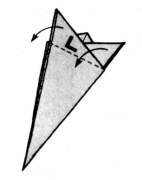

5 Overlap the front flaps and glue them together. Fold the top corners forward.

6 Glue two units together as shown. Then join the remaining units, as shown in step **7**.

7 The gentian completed.

What about making a gentian brooch? Fold two flowers, using 5 cm. (2 in.) squares of paper. Slip a loop of embroidery thread between the units when you stick them together, and then hang them from a safety pin.

58

Hanging decoration

If you make this model on a large scale, it will serve as a room decoration. If you make a miniature one, it can be used as a mascot to hang in a car. Thirty sheets are used.

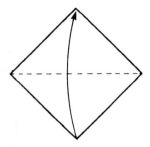

1 With the plain side up, fold in half.

2 Fold the bottom corners to the top.

×30

3 One unit completed. Fold a total of thirty units in the same way.

4 Overlap the front flaps and glue them together.

5 Make sure you don't spoil the roundness of the far side.

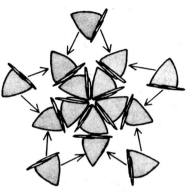

6 When you've glued the individual units, join five of them in a ring as shown.

7 Join five more units to the ring. Next, prepare another five units by applying glue to two faces of each. Fix them around the ring as shown.

8 One half of the decoration is completed. Make the other half by repeating steps **6** and **7** with the remaining fifteen units.

9 Make a loop of embroidery thread. Tie a bunch of threads to one end of it to form a tassel. Glue the two halves of the decoration together with the loop between them so that the tassel hangs from it.

10 The decoration completed.

59

Musical models

The following three or four models are meant to be folded in time to music. In the original Japanese edition of this book, each item is presented with a few lines of music and verses for singing while folding. That's why the yacht, for example, has such large, sweeping movements. Without the music, this may seem a bit strange, but you could always try singing songs you know while you fold. It might bring you closer to the Japanese spirit of origami!

The yacht

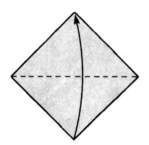

1 With the coloured side up, fold two corners together.

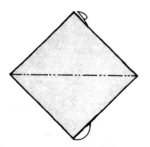

3 Now mountain fold the corners together.

2 Unfold.

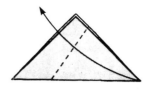

4 Fold up the bottom right corner as shown. Rotate the paper . . .

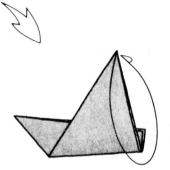

5 . . . like this. Now swing the front flap down, around and up behind.

6 Take the flap down again and reverse fold it up between the layers to form a sail.

7 The yacht completed.

The plane

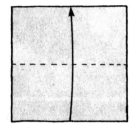

1 With the coloured side up, fold two edges together.

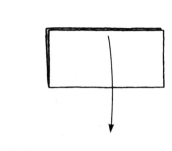

2 Open up.

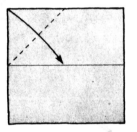

3 Fold one corner to the crease line . . .

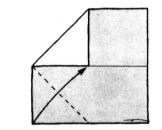

4 . . . and fold another corner to the crease line . . .

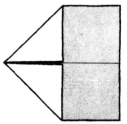

5 . . . like this. Turn the paper over.

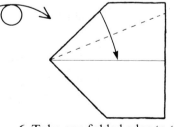

6 Take one folded edge to the crease line . . .

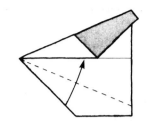

7 . . . and the other folded edge to the crease line . . .

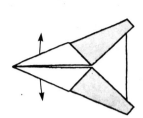

8 . . . like this. Pull the loose corners from behind.

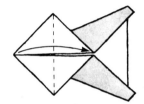

9 Fold the white square area in half.

10 Mountain fold the model in half.

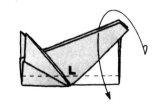

11 Fold the front and rear flaps to front and back to stand out at right-angles to the model.

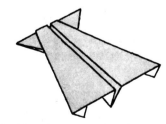

12 The plane completed.

Yakko-san and his trousers

Yakko-san is a traditional large-headed Japanese clown. The first model represents him wearing a skirted and wide-sleeved kimono. Slip trousers on to this model to make a differently proportioned figure.

Yakko-san

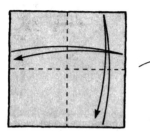

1 With the coloured side up, fold opposite edges of the paper together in turn. Turn the paper over.

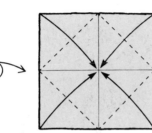

2 Blintz fold.

3 Turn the paper over.

4 Blintz fold again.

5 Turn over.

6 Blintz fold for the third time.

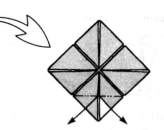

7 Turn over.

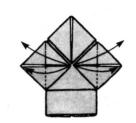

8 At the bottom, open the flap by pulling the two edges apart, allowing the point to spread and come down . . .

9 . . . like this. Fold the side flaps in half, at the same time raising the upper edges . . .

10 . . . like this. Yakko-san is completed.

His trousers

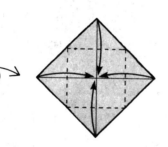

1 Repeat steps **1–10**, then open up the top and side flaps so that all four corner flaps are similar. Next, unfold the sides . . .

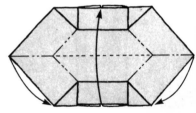

2 . . . like this. Pinch the sides as you fold the bottom to the top . . .

3 . . . like this. Yakko-san's trousers are completed.

Ideas page

Hydrangea wall hanging

Let's make a hydrangea wall hanging from the *'leaf'* bookmark (page 35), and the *hanging decoration* (page 59). Pick suitably coloured papers for making the leaves and flowers.

What you need

four 'leaf' bookmarks
two halves of the hanging decoration (unjoined)
one empty cardboard box
one piece of string
glue
coloured paper, about 30 cm. (12 in.) square

2 Lightly mark the places where the halves of the hanging decoration are to be fixed.

4 Glue each half of the hanging decoration in place.

How to make the wall hanging

1 Cover the box with coloured paper. Run a piece of string through the top.

3 Shape the 'leaf' bookmarks so that they are a bit rounded and glue them in place.

It's a pretty wall decoration, isn't it? It would make a fine present too.

Index of folds

The following signs, symbols, words and phrases are introduced and explained on the pages shown.